# 1 Hour per Day Social Media Guide

— e-book —

Timer
60 min

0

45

15

30

## 1 Hour Per Day Social Media Guide

### By Pat Hopper

Your guide to building a community using
Facebook, LinkedIn, Twitter, Pinterest and More

# 1 Hour per Day Social Media Guide

Chapter 1: My Story

Chapter 2: A Few Rules before we get started

Chapter 3: Twitter

Chapter 4: Facebook

Chapter 5: LinkedIn

Chapter 6: Pinterest/Instagram

Chapter 7: Groupon/ Living Social

Chapter 8: FourSquare

Chapter 9: Tying it all Together

Chapter 10: About the Author

# Chapter 1: My Story

The following book is a great resource for anyone looking to explore social media to build a community. I did it, I have no special skills, I made lots of mistakes, but over a 4 year period I built a network of over 13,000 followers, took on established media print and online publishers and won. I only invested under $1000 of capital and one hour per day. And, I did it twice.

Get ready to have fun and learn a lot. I have provided all the tips, tricks and software that was very useful to me. Hope you enjoy!

### *My Story*

This is my story. It is the story about being a little inquisitive, trying everything, commiting to making mistakes and trying to find success from the ashes.

Starting my communities began with hard work, lots of networking, lots of trials and many errors. I really do not possess too many extra ordinary skills except for my passion for new technologies and to build a community that serves itself. I know very little HTML, I don't have any graphics capabilities, and I didn't spend much money.

I used gorilla marketing techniques required with minimal budgets, partnered with everyone I find. I was not afraid to try something new, make a call or send an email. I have made countless speaches, presented at tradeshows, met with competitors, brainstormed with industry leaders and listened and learned from everyone I could find.

It began in 2007 when I started attending some local social media events lead by Terry Bean and Charlie Curve in the metro-Detroit area. Their classes gave me many useful tools and I began to integrate with my publishing company, OpenSystems Media, to drive new subscribers, generate leads and build our brands. I started writing down the techniques I learned and read about (Twitter Power, etc). That soon lead to writing a whitepaper (really just a really rough shared document on google that I wrote). I soon had over 6,000 downloads and soon became a social media expert in the electronics industry. I now manage 6 twitter accounts, I am member of 50 groups on LinkedIn, manage 10 groups on LinkedIn and have build our magazines brands in our electronics community.

I then start thinking; where else could I apply the things I have learned. My first thought was… wouldn't it be cool to be able to drive flash mobs to a location via social media and charge the vendor for that coverage. My community that I live in is Grosse Pointe, Michigan, an upper middle class suberb of Detroit.

So, I began to think of possible names for my new venture, keeping in mind that I needed to have a consistant user names with all the accounts and a possible web site down the line. I came up with Grosse Pointey mainly because the Twitter account was open, a gmail account was available (grossepointey@gmail.com) and domain was available for sale. Other variations of the name Grosse Pointe all seemed to be taken.

I then created a very basic twitter account, made about a hundred bumper stickers and started my new venture. I followed everyone in Grosse Pointe, attended Grosse Pointe Chamber meetings, did Lunch and Learns with local businesses and found out only about 400 people in all Grosse Pointe were on Twitter. During this time, I started honing my news aggregator skills, created "auto follow back set ups" and integrated an RSS feed to the Twitter account to deliver news without me manually doing it.

I then decided I needed to move my message to Facebook. I actually created a user name Grosse Pointey and then created a Group and Fan Page. I started with my personal account of randomly befriending local people and posting news stories about school closings, news stories, fires, community events, live and in realtime. In March of 2008, I had about 90 friends and 25 people on the fan page. At this time, I was on a conference call at my office and in boredom, logged onto Facebook, found the high school Mom's Club and befriended all the moms and then made posts about upcoming school events.

Then it got exciting.

In the next 6 months, I went from 90 friends to 1000, then to 2000, 3000 and finally to 5000 (which is the facebook maximum), the group and fan pages topped 1700 each, I got in to FourSquare, Pinterest, Flickr, LinkedIn and any social media site I could create an account with. I added a web site, synced them all together and then started thinking of ways to drive revenue. I contacted the local paper, worked with community groups and even hired a marketing person to help. After 3 years, our coverage on social media sites topped 13,000 engaged users, topping the local paper and all other media forms in my area.

The following E-book will help you do the same.  I will walk you through exactly which accounts to open, how to sync them together, what programs to use, strategies, and ways to drive revenue.  You don't need any special skills and really only need a cell phone and a laptop.  You can take on the media giants, create a nich and win in only 1 hour per day.

In order to minimize your time, you will need to maximize all your posts.  I will also show you how to post once and populate across your socia media platforms.

Pats' Tip: Before you start, download Dropbox to your computer and smart phone.  Then, create a document with all your user names and passwords.  When you begin your social media journal, forgetting your password should be an issue.

Pat's Tip:  As you begin using social media, keep in mind you are creating a brand, the brand could be you.  Everything you do should be about enhancing your personal brand optimization.

# Chapter 2:  A few Rules before We Get Started

1) Early Adopters Win.  You must take the first step, develop your brand and begin the process.  Do not be afraid to fail.
2) Join all participate in a few.  Join as many groups, social media sites as you can, secure your company names, but only participate in the few you understand.
3) Focus on LinkedIn, Twitter and Facebook.  These are the key social media outlets.  Spend your 1 hour per day on these sites.
4) Personal Brand Optimization.  Your goal is to be an expert in your desired field or community.  All your sites and branding should reflect your goal.
5) Use social media to create and build relationships and to expand your business outside of your current clientele.
6) Feed your network.  Comment on news, articles, and PR daily.  Measure your comments and links.
7) Determine what times and days are best to post and what posts your community likes to see.  Measure as many posts as you can.
8) Be consistent.  Your LinkedIn, Twitter and Facebook accounts should all provide your message.
9) Stay visible.
10) 7:1 ratio.   Post 7 times about general market trends before you talk about yourself or your company.
11) Must be timely and responsive

NOTE: Input from this book was derived from vast research plus Terry Bean, Charlie Wollberg, *Twitter Power* by Joel Comm, *The $100 Start Up* by Chris Guillebeau, and *Crush It!* By Gary Vaynerchuk.

# Chapter 3: Twitter

Twitter was the first social media site I really explored.  It is fun and simple to use.

## Background

There are a few key things you need to know 1) Posts are only 140 characters long.  This coincides with the maximum size of a text message via your cell phone.  Twitter was built with the mobile market in mind. 2) You should consider using a link shortening tool incase you are posting articles or news (since many times your link could contain 140 characters.  3) Despite the fact that Twitter was designed for mobile use, do not use the same characters if you were texting.  You should not use LOL or C U L8TR.  4) Twitter enables you to create a profile and a great background.  I recommend getting a professional designer for your creation.

A few other thoughts on Twitter

1) You can follow anyone you wish, there is no recprocity
2) I would suggest following 25-50 people at a time talking about your interests, then waiting for them to follow you back.  On average 30-50% of the people you follow will follow you back.
3) You should follow everyone that follows you (assuming there is not a spam type person following you).
4) If you post something and you immediately get more followers, it could be due to several keywords you used in your post
5) Recognize that there are people out there searching keywords.  When you use those keywords, people automatically will begin to follow you, so watch out!

## Account Creation

Creating an account is easy.  I would try to layout your vision before starting an account so you can begin to have a unified message across many social media platforms.   Your Facebook, LinkedIn, web site, email, Twitter and Pinterest accounts should all be consistant.  When creating your bio, feel free to get a bit zaney.  Many people suggest using a strategy such as: first name, job, passion, and then a little comic relief.  Here are some of my favorites

**Charlie Wollborg**
@CharlieCurve
*Chief Troublemaker. Creative. Marketer. Entrepreneur. Speaker. I love shiny objects bacon & business. On a mission to rekindle the fire in your belly*
Detroit, Michigan   http://www.charliecurve.com

**Terry Bean**
@terrybean
*I am far more interested in you than I will ever be in me. Author. Pro Speaker. Disruptive Marketing Force @MotorCity Founder. Detroit Lover. 248.224.1326*
Detroit   http://unetworked.com

You should spend some time developing a background.  I have used Tweetpages.com which was very economical.   Here are some cool sites to check out:

## Demographics

Median age 31, typically hip urban people.  Largest demographics are 18-35 year olds, 53% female and 47% male.  A typically Twitter user would well connected to the world via their mobile device.

## Software to implement

I use Hootsuite for my computer and the Twitter application for my iphone.  Hootsuite allows you to manage multiple accounts, has a build in link shortener, and allows you to watch and track keywords across the web.  It also allows you to schedule your tweets.  Tracking keywords is key for a community.  If you want to build your community, you need to do the following

1) Who are the key players already there (are there stores, restaurants, key people, politicians, charities)
2) Try to begin to interact with them.  On Fridays, you should do a #FF post on Twitter (see details below)
3) If people are talking about a topic, jump in with your input

*SocialOomph.com.* I use SocialOomph to return follow everyone that follows me and I use it to send a welcome message to everyone who follows me.   You can see my welcome message below.

*TweetAdder* is a great tool. It allows you to follow people based on a term in their bio, or a word in their tweets. So, if you wanted to follow everyone in Detroit, simply tell TweetAdder to search bio for Detroit and follow them. You can also use this tool to unfollow people that are not following you.

*TwitterFeed* is a tool to sync your account with an RSS news feed. RSS stands for Real Simple Syndication. If you wish to have news automatically populate your Twitter account, you can use this useful software for this. To get a link for your news feed, go to www.google.com/news. Type in your search term and ensure you have provided enough keywords, then click search. At the bottom of the page you will see a RSS button. Click on that and it should give you the link to the google RSS feed that you can use with Twitterfeed.

Tip: Use Twitterfeed in the beginning so it helps populate your timeline.

### *Etiquette*
Since Twitter allows you to follow anyone you wish, you do not want your profile to appear you are following lots of people and no one cares about following you back. So, follow 25-50 people at a time, wait for them to follow you back then follow more. Also, once you follow 2000 people, you cannot follow anymore until the number of people catch up to you and then you can only follow in 10% increments. Thus, if I follow 2200 people and 2000 people are following me, I cannot follow anymore until someone new follows me.

Also, you should not post several article or tweets in a row. Use Hootsuite to schedule your tweets.

Tip: Use TweetAdder to unfollow the 200 people that are not following you back so you can follow 200 more.

## Key terms

\# hashtag.  A hashtag is a way for people to follow a certain event or news item by placing the # hashtag before or after your post.  Some of the most popular hashtags of 2011 were

1) #egypt
2) #tigerblood (thank Charlie Sheen for this one)
3) #superbowl
4) #jan25 (relating to Egypt's revolution)
5) #threewordstoliveby
6) #FF (follow Friday- very key)
7) You can develop your own #hashtag too, just start using it!

DM.  A DM is a direct message that only you and the recipient can view

RT or Retweek.  Is a lazy mans tool for posting.  You can retweet someone elses tweet.  This is a good tool if you are trying to connect with an industry leader.

## Syncing

Twitter can easily sync to your LinkedIn profile, so every post can be populated across three plaforms.  See LinkedIn on how to do this.

To Link your Twitter account to your Facebook Profile, click on Settings, then Profile.  See image below.

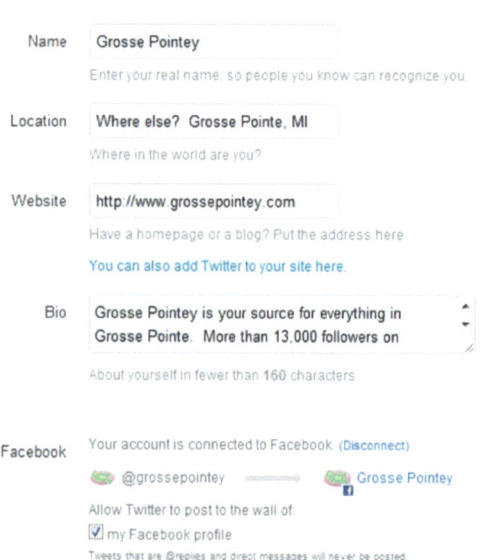

## How to find people

If you want to search people or topics, go to http://search.twitter.com and begin following relevant people.

## Strategies

When developing your online presence, you need to begin thinking of yourself as the thought leader in your community. Thus, you will need to follow everyone in your community, engage with them, attend local tradeshows, events, and chamber meetings, and join social media organizations and aggregate news to your community.

I would start posting a relevant article to your community on Twitter. I would then work on your bio and your background. I would then use http://search.twitter.com and begin following relevant people. Follow 25-50 at a time to ensure your Followers vs Following ratio is pretty even.

Next I would set up an account on *SocialOomph* (free) to follow anyone back that follows you and you create a welcome message to your community. In your welcome message you could include a custom hashtag you want to use, direct people to a Facebook Fan Page or your web site. Note, your welcome message is 140 characters too.

Finally, I would set up your *Hootsuite* Account. I would create "streams" so you can follow keywords and hashtags. Everytime you see someone mentioning those words, follow them, or if relevant to your audience, RT it. You should post 3-7x per week.

If your community has a tradeshow or event, watch for people discussing it on Twitter. You don't even need to be at the event to make a presence.

Set up TwitterFeed and sync your news feed with a twitter account. This allows for relevant news with your keywords to automatically fill in your timeline. NOTE: Only do this once per day. Many people on Twitter don't like blatant news feeds without commentary.

Finally, get a little sassy, zaney or kooky. Don't just post news, add a comment.

## Measuring your posts

You will need to determine which posts work and which do not. Hootsuite has a neat link shortening tool that allows you to grab large links, shrink them and track them to see which work.  You can also use www.bit.ly.

Pat's Tip:  Your first tweet should not be "I just opened a Twitter account".  Post an interesting article.

Pat's Tricks: Follow people that are relevant.  Ask questions and even be a little bit controversial to get followers.  Link as many items to your Facebook Fanpage or your website.  I created a "How to Guide" that I retweeted that estabished me as an industry expert.  I made an industry list of top people to follow on Twitter and what the popular hashtags were.  Vendors soon began to email me asking to be included in the list.  I could then send a Tweet saying I recently added @xyz to my list of "Who to follow"

# Chapter 4: Facebook

### Background

Facebook is the 800 pound gorilla and is the most widely used platform on the social web. Most businesses should have a fan page to keep their clients informed. Vendors that do it well have contests, invest in nice graphics and welcome images and encourage people to post and interact with other fans.

### Demographics

The shear numbers of people on Facebook make this social media platform a must. Currently over 900 million people are active users and with roughly 100 million in the United States. The average user spends about 15 hours per month on this site. It is crutial to creatively engage with your network. About 70% of the people using Facebook at 13-35 and it are split fairly evenly between male and female.

### Account Creation

Creating a Facebook account is easly. You will need to create a personal account before you can create a fan page. Once your page is created, do some browsing. See what other similar vendors are doing. You can "like" their pages and when they update, you will be able to track their updates.

When you are ready, go to this link: http://www.facebook.com/pages/create.php

 Create a Page
Create a Facebook Page to build a closer relationship with your audience and customers.

 Pages I Like | Pages I Admin

Local Business or Place

Company, Organization or Institution

Brand or Product

Artist, Band or Public Figure

Entertainment

Cause or Community

You will have the update to add your logo, location, business hours, website, phone number and all relevant details. You can now begin posting relevant news, specials, and updates to your fan page. Some words of caution

1) Use the 7:1 ratio on your fan page. Comment 7 times on news items, cool ideas, and great articles before commenting on yourself. Very few people will sign up for a fan page that only promotes them.
2) Add photos whenever possible
3) Add videos whenever possible

NOTE: The new image size of the fan page photo is 851 x 351, so get creative and use a cool image for your main image.

### Fan Page Insights
Insights is the fan page tool tracking the statistics on the page. It is very useful!

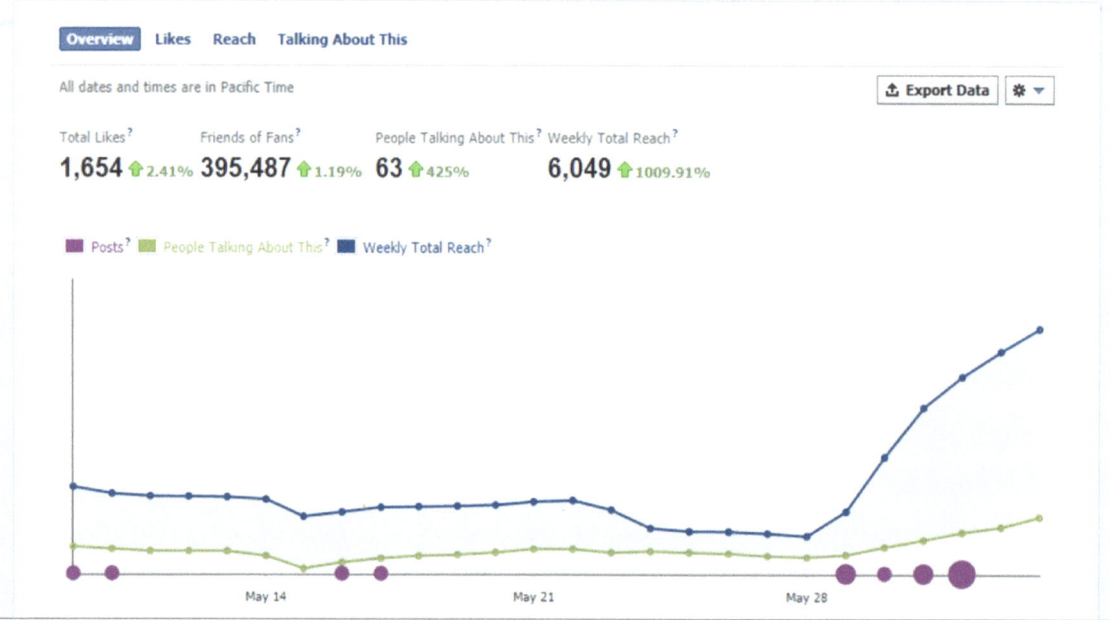

You can also see which comments had the most traction.

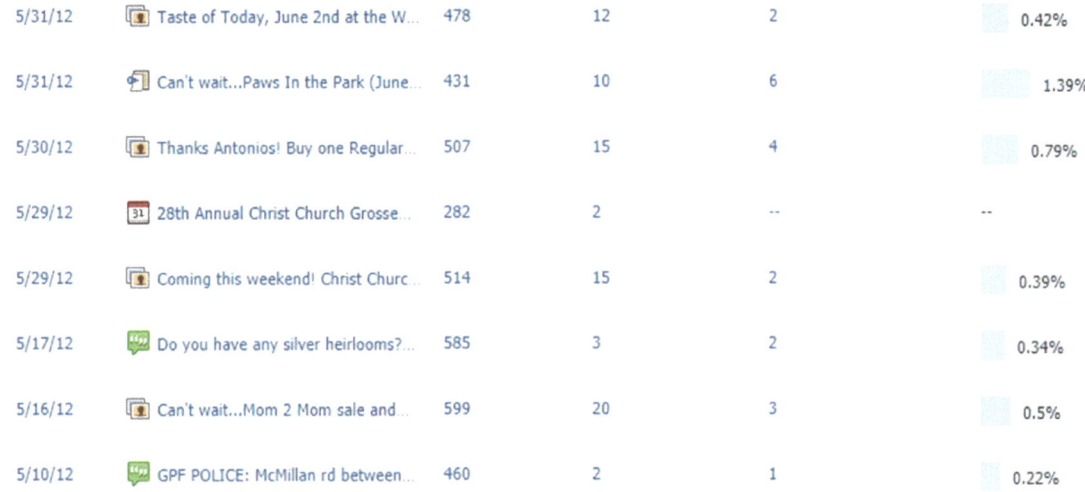

| Date | | Views | Comments | Shares | Rate |
|---|---|---|---|---|---|
| 5/31/12 | Taste of Today, June 2nd at the W... | 478 | 12 | 2 | 0.42% |
| 5/31/12 | Can't wait...Paws In the Park (June... | 431 | 10 | 6 | 1.39% |
| 5/30/12 | Thanks Antonios! Buy one Regular... | 507 | 15 | 4 | 0.79% |
| 5/29/12 | 28th Annual Christ Church Grosse... | 282 | 2 | -- | -- |
| 5/29/12 | Coming this weekend! Christ Churc... | 514 | 15 | 2 | 0.39% |
| 5/17/12 | Do you have any silver heirlooms?... | 585 | 3 | 2 | 0.34% |
| 5/16/12 | Can't wait...Mom 2 Mom sale and... | 599 | 20 | 3 | 0.5% |
| 5/10/12 | GPF POLICE: McMillan rd between... | 460 | 2 | 1 | 0.22% |

Here are a few tips:

1) Encourage customers to "like" your page
2) Add your fanpage URL to your receipts, email signature and stationary
3) Use Insights to guage the effectiveness of your posts

### Syncing with Twitter(1 post, 2 locations)

You can sync your Facebook Fan Page and your Twitter page by going here:
http://www.facebook.com/twitter/

### Buying Ads on Facebook

If you wish to purchase ads on Facebook to promote your site, it is easily done.  Typically in the right column of your home page you will see a column with a sponsored message

and an opportunity to create an ad.    Sponsored     Create an Ad

When creating your ad you can select different types of ads and then where to target. You can target by location, demographics and activities, and then set up a budget.

Tips:

1) Facebook ads typically receive half the click through rates of regular banners or .05%, so monitor your effectiveness.
2) Facebook will want you target a larger audience to deliver your message

3) Remember, you will be competing with larger brands targeting your space
4) When directing people to your Fan Page, make sure you logo is appealing and your words are creative.

Facebook provides some really neat stats.

| | Name | Status | Reach | Freq. | Social Reach | Actions | Clicks | CTR | Bid | Price |
|---|---|---|---|---|---|---|---|---|---|---|
| | Grosse Pointey | ▶ ▼ | 4,572 | 11.4 | 4,572 | 310 | 125 | 0.241% | $0.78 CPC | $0.30 CPC |

## *Software Integration*
You can easily sync your Facebook fanpage with your twitter account so all posts you do to your fanpage automatically flow into your twitter account.  Simply follow the link below:
http://www.facebook.com/twitter/

## *Etiquette*
There is a tendancy on Facebook to drive traffic to your fan page and then to innundate them with special offers from your compay.  Do not do this.  Use the 7:1 ratio to posting about industry related events and then insert your advertising message in less frequently.

## *Strategies*
When making your posts, you should consistant when your followers will be online.  If you are targeting a business class, you may wish to post during lunch hour.  If you are targeting students, then 4:30.  For mothers, I typically suggest 9am, noon, 4 or 7pm.

Pat's Tip: Since your posts sync from Facebook fan page to Twitter, you should make then 140 characters or less.

Pat's Tip:  Remember to measure all your posts to determine which posts and times work.

Pat's Tricks:  You can create a custom HTML welcome page to your FanPage.  You can also ask people to "share" the page to encourage more followers.

# Chapter 5: LinkedIn

LinkedIn is the most important business networking site.  There are roughly 150 million users (about 60% male), ages 25-54.  This is a group of savvy networkers with a media income of over $100k.  This is the number one spot to enhance your brand, cultivate it, and watch it grow.  From your profile to your posts, you should always be thinking how it improves your brand.

## *Profile*

The first step with LinkedIn is your profile.  You will need to include a professionally done photo.  Do not use a photo taken by yourself or with a confusing background.  Some creative images to add instrant credibility include photos taken while giving a presentation during a trade conference, holding a microphone, with a flag in the background, taken in black and white.  Your photo should accurately reflect who you are and what you are trying to portray.

I have included my profile below.  I also added my phone (added after last name on "edit" profile section.  I also included many keywords so if people are searching, my name will appear under many different areas.

## Patrick Hopper (586-484-5964) Edit

Publisher | Partner | Influencer | Social Media Guru |
Embedded/Military Marketing and Web 2.0 Strategist.

Greater Detroit Area  |  Publishing

LinkedIn "likes" when you fill out your profile completely and will give you a percentage rank as to how much you have completed.  The more jobs, schooling/education, websites, etc your provide, the greater the percentage.

There is also an area for your summary.  See below.  I added many of my professional skills, some comments about my personal life (this is OK) and even a zaney sentence that I had copied from another profile (I am happily married to my unhappily married wife, Kate).  I am a pretty light hearted guy and I am hoping to drive a few smirks when someone reads this.  This is another area that should be chalked full of keywords and phrases that are relevant in your industry.

The summary area also allows you to add "skills", publications (if you have ever writen), books you are reading, events you are attending and more.  You should do your best to fill out all areas.

There is an area called Applications.  This allows you to add cool applications like the Amazon Books you are reading (make sure the books you are reading give you credibility and match your profile), Slideshare, Polls, Travel and more.  The more areas you add to your profile, the more credibility you will have and the more your profile will be searched when people are looking for other contacts.

## Summary  Edit

Professional:
I am the Publisher/Partner and social media guru at OpenSystems Media. I consult with almost every major vendor in the embedded marketplace on strategic campaigns involving lead generation, social media engagement, print, online, apps, channels and blogging.

I am here to help.

I am also a speaker/panelists at several Embedded conferences and the author of "Using Twitter and Linkedin in the Embedded marketplace." To date there have been more than 6,000 downloads.
Click here to download your copy: http://bit.ly/BECRd

Personal:
I enjoy playing tennis, coaching baseball, spending time with friends and family. I have two great kids, Patrick Jr and Caroline. I am happily married to my unhappily married wife, Kate.

Specialties
Print and online media, social networking, technology, twitter/facebook/linkedin, lead generation, embedded systems, apps, webcasting.

### Creating a custom URL in LinkedIn
If you click on Profile – Edit and scroll down to the bottom of your main profile box, you will see a link to the URL of your public profile:

Public Profile    http://www.linkedin.com/in/patrickhopper  Edit

If you click on the edit button, you can customize your profile URL and replace the current one with your name.

After you have your customized link, make sure to feature it on your signature in your email.  See my signature below:

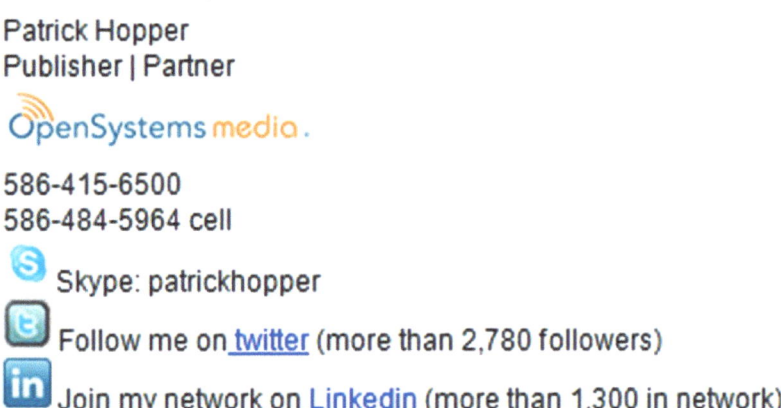

Patrick Hopper
Publisher | Partner

OpenSystems media.

586-415-6500
586-484-5964 cell

Skype: patrickhopper

Follow me on twitter (more than 2,780 followers)

Join my network on Linkedin (more than 1,300 in network)

Posting and Syncing to Twitter (1 post, 2 locations)

LinkedIn provides a spot on your homescreen to post your relevant news comments on articles.  You can include a link directly to an article you are commenting on.  Everyone who is connected will see your post scroll through their home screen.  Thus, the more followers you have, the more opportunities you have to position yourself as an industry leader.

If you would like your post Sync'd with Twitter, click on the small bird below.  Please ensure that your post to no greater than 140 characters or else it will be truncated on Twitter.

OpenSystems Media is a full service media company......  · Like (2)  · Comment (2)  · More »  · 5 days ago

## Groups

One of the best ways to connect with other like minded people or to engage with an audience is through Groups. There are literally thousands of groups that you can join and track and monitor what is going on in your industry.

The key to groups is to not only join and monitor/interact with discussions, but weekly post an interesting article to that group. The more you post, the more credibility you will have on your desired topic. Many of the groups contain thousands of potential leads. LinkedIn allows you to join 50 groups and manage 10. You will want to manage your group settings to ensure you do not receive daily emails from group. I suggest updating your settings to weekly. See screen shot below for details.

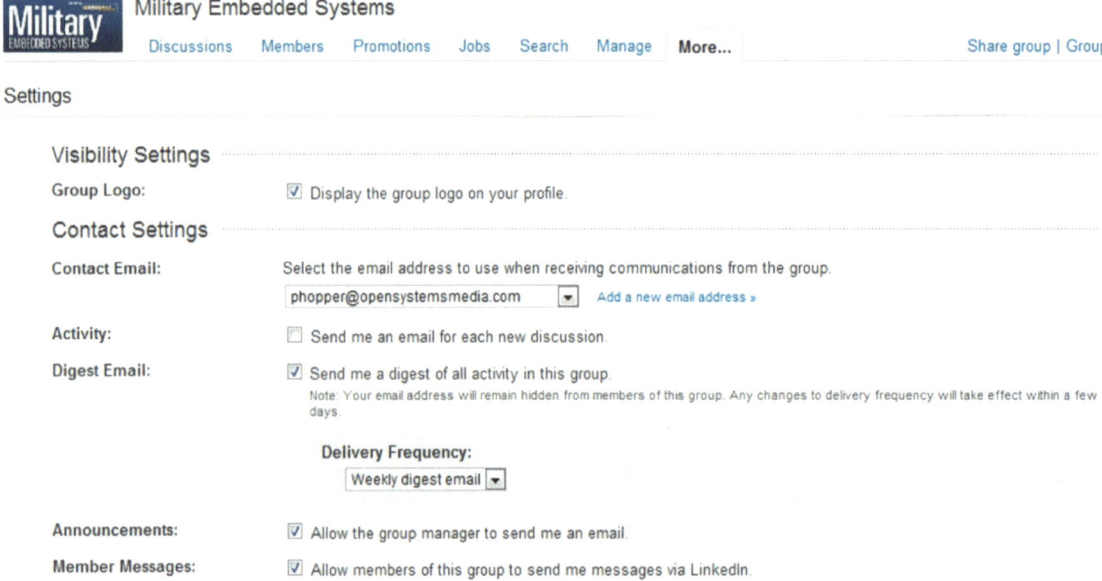

You can also create a group. I suggest the following when creating a group

1) Make it an industry group vs your company group. If you were targeting CFO's create a new group entitled CFO Network or if you were building a local community of business leaders you could call it the {insert city name} Networking Group.

2) "Owning" a group allow you to weekly email the group. Remember the 7:1 ratio. If you post weekly sales items, people will leave the group. If you post relevant

content people will join.  To send an announcement, click on Manage→ Send an Announcement.

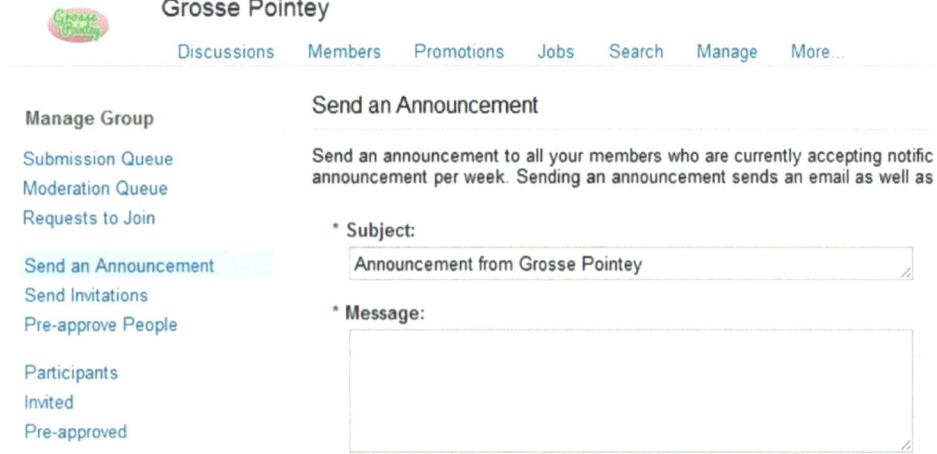

3) You can also add a news feed to your group.  Your news feed can be from your web site or from your Twitter account.  In order to add your Twitter feed as a news source for your group do the following:

   a.  Go to http://api.twitter.com/users/show/username
   b.  Find the numeric id for that user

   ```
   <user>
     <id>15612771</id>
     <name>Patrick Hopper</name>
     <screen_name>patrickhopper</screen_name>
     <location>Detroit, MI</location>
   ```

   c.  http://twitter.com/statuses/user_timeline/XXXXX.rss **Replace the XXXX with 15612771.  Cop the entire link.**
   d.  **Next go your Group- Manage- News Feeds and paste the link.**

## Who to Follow

I make it a point to follow everyone in either my community or in marketing or upper management with any company I work with.  I even follow all of my competitors.  LinkedIn has a great algorithm that shows you who they they you should be connected with.  If you look on your home tab, on the right hand side lists several people.  You may click more to see an entire list.

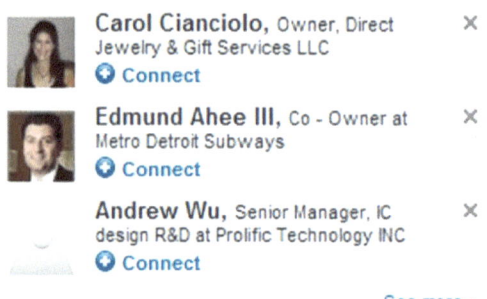

**People You May Know**

Carol Cianciolo, Owner, Direct
Jewelry & Gift Services LLC
Connect

Edmund Ahee III, Co - Owner at
Metro Detroit Subways
Connect

Andrew Wu, Senior Manager, IC
design R&D at Prolific Technology INC
Connect

See more »

Caution- Words of Wisdom

1) If you try to connect with too many people that do not know you, LinkedIn may require you to provide an email address. So be careful and make sure you are connecting with the right people.

2) DO NOT USE THE STANDARD LINKED MESSAGE. Create your own. LinkedIn automatically populates the invitation with: I'd like to add you to my professional network. Do not use this. This is a great opportunity to add a clever message such as, "Hi Bill, I'd like to invite you to my (XYZ) network on LinkedIn. As an industry expert, I love to keep my network informed, Thanks!"

### *Privacy*

If you are concerned that your competitors may be watching your account to see who you are connecting with, you can change your settings to ensure only the people you want to see your updates, do.

Click on your name on the top right. Then click settings. You can elect that everyone sees your updates, your network, your connections or only you.

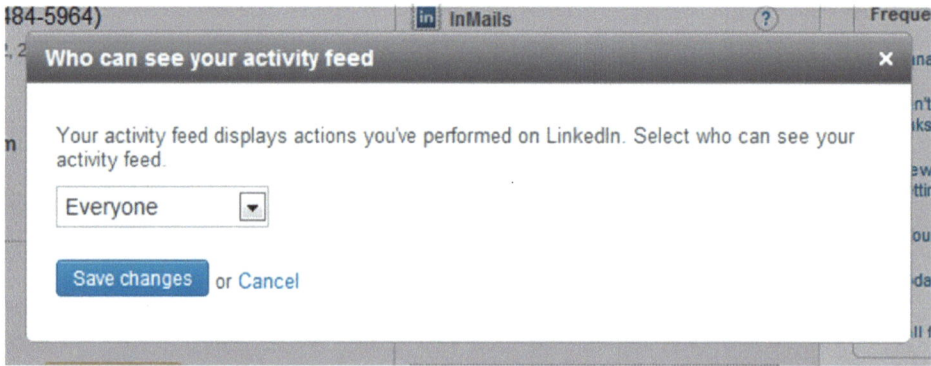

Pats Tip:  If you see a large group, contact the owner of the group and ask if you can help "manage" the group.  If they allow you to do this, then you can send announcements to the group.  Many group owners have created the group years ago and no longer have the same job, thus many of them look for assistance.

Pat's Tip:  Come to grips with this, your resume is no longer of value.  Your LinkedIn profile is now your current resume.

Pat's Tricks:  In the drop down menu under "More" there is an "Answers" link.  Answer as many questions in your field to improve your brand.

Also, try going to http://www.linkedin.com/signal/ .  This tool allows you to easily monitor your connections and what they are doing.

Exporting contacts.  If you click on my contacts, at the bottom right of that page is an export feature.  This will easily allow you to get all your contacts email addresses.

# Chapter 6: Pinterest/Instagram

Pinterest and other photo sharing sites such as Instagram are popping up all over the place. They are predominantly followed by women (about 80%) and the ages are 24-50.

Pinterest allows their followers to boards on their site and on each board there are pins of popular pictures. A typical board may include folders such as My Fashion, Recipes, Places I want to Visit, Home Style and more. Users simply fill the boards with the photos that interest them and then download the App to their iPhone or Android device to access later.

If you own a store or run a community where photos are important, this is the site for you. You are easily snap photos, upload them to your board and your followers can "like" your photo or "repin" to their site. 20 million users spend a whopping 14 minutes per day checking out photos.

### *Here is how to make it cool*

1) You can invite friends from your gmail, Facebook or Yahoo account
2) You can search boards in your community and follow their pins. You can search by people or by boards.
3) You can share your photos on Facebook and Twitter (click under settings)

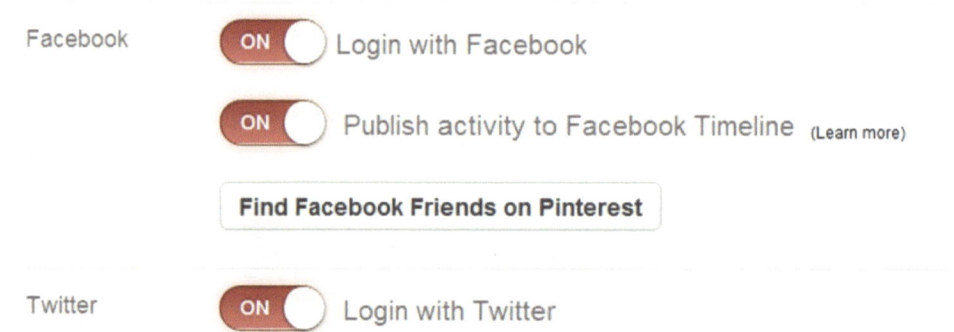

4) You can find friends on Facebook

The goal is to post new photos of your products, services or your community event each day. If you are targeting "soccer moms" and students, this is a perfect way to engage. Also, realtors, interior designers, restuarants, caterers, chambers of commerce are other great people to use this service.

Photos should be colorful and unique.

Pats Tip:  When you post your new pins, make sure to describe them using keywords people in your industry use.

Pats Tip: Try posting great quotes with your photos.

Pats Tip: Follow everyone in your area, repin other photos to encourage others to do the same for you.

Pat's Tricks:  Try using http://www.pinwords.com/ and add words to your images to make them "pop".  Also, download PinSearch.com which allows you to search like images on Pinterest (see search icon on image).

# Chapter 7: Groupon and Living Social

Groupon and LivingSocial are the premier coupon sites and are two good sources for retailers and service companies to drive more traffic. They usually involve a 30-70% discounted coupon and a time frame to buy and use the coupon. Both of these sites are dominated by woman (roughly 70%) with a media age of 18-34.

Groupon had at one point a larger presence in the mid-west and LivingSocial at one pointe had a largest presence in the south. Both are now full integrated nationally. LivingSocial has more emphasis places and Groupon has more emphasis on restaurants and services.

Although their reach in various communities is huge, there are some draw backs. The pay out plan that Groupon keeps 50% of the coupon and pay you 33% in the first month, 33% in the second month and 33% in the third month. So, if your coupon generates $10,000, they pay you $5000 over the next three months. For a service industry, you may be doing a lot of work at low wages with non-recurring clients. Many restuaurants use Groupon to drive people into the restuaurant where they can make more money of liquor sales.

You can also earn Groupon bucks to use to pay for your own Groupons. I routinely promote Groupons in my area across Facebook, Twitter and LinkedIn. If someone buys my Groupon using the link I provided, I receive $10 in Groupon bucks. Or you can refer a friend and earn $10 in Groupon bucks. I have earned over $500 in Groupon bucks by promoting local offers.

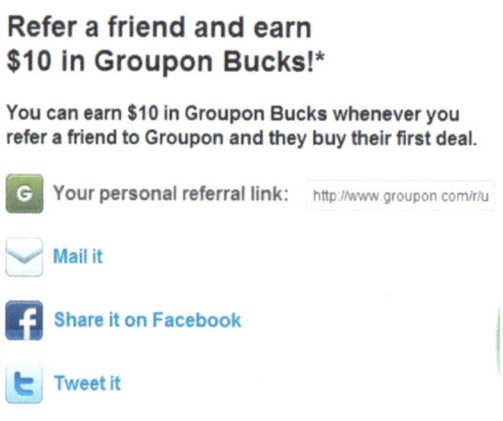

# Chapter 8: FourSquare

FourSquare is a free app that allows you to touch base with your friends by "checking in" at different locations. Roughly 60% of the users are male, ages 24-35 and about 20 million users routinely "check in".

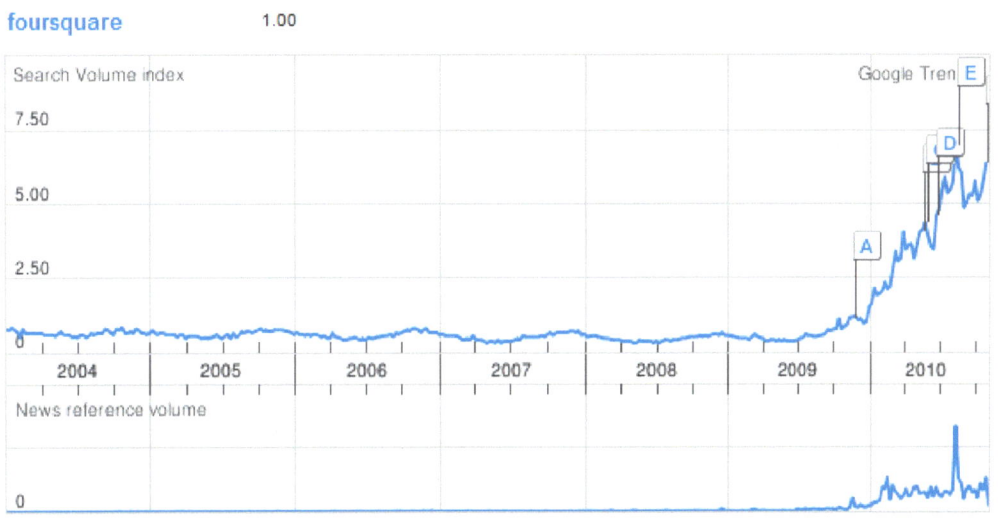

This is a very popular tool if you have a store front, restaurant or a physical location you encourage your clients to visit. When people "check in" they can become the "Mayor" of your location. Many shops and coffee houses reward the mayor with certain perks to try to encourage others to check in and dethrown the current mayor. The mayor may keep his status if he leads with check-ins. The more you check in, the more you earn badges.

You can also provide tips at various locations or specials for visitors who check in, you can find the "top picks" that are near you. You can also follow anyone in your community and see where they are checking in.

Most major metropolitan areas have a huge FourSquare following. The smaller communities are much more difficult since it is an emerging social account.

Pats Tips: I suggest at least starting an account and explore your area to see if there are people searching your types of business. Leave as many tips as you can in your area. I suggest also following everyone in your area, rewarding the Mayor if you have a retail establishment and offering specials for those that check in.

<u>Pat's Tricks</u>:  You can sync your FourSquare account with your Facebook page and your Twitter account.  Post once, populate in several places.

I also suggest posting photos.  What a great way to show off your storefront!

# Chapter 9: Tying it all Together

The key to this book is to develop a presence on social media outlets and then tie together.  If you can create one post, and populate two social media outlets, you have done this successfully.

Here are the key areas to tie together to maximize exposure and reduce time.

1) LinkedIn posts and Twitter tweets
2) Twitter Tweets and Facebook posts
3) Facebook Fan Page posts to Twitter Tweets
4) Pinterest Pins and Facebook home page
5) Groupon Share with Facebook and Twitter

In order to minimize your time posting, use the above methods to sync all your accounts.

Building a community takes time and hard work.  In the early stages you will need to slot one hour per day to get your community, business, retail store or services running.  But, the hours you spend at the beginning make your life easier after a few weeks.  People will begin to seek you out, use you as a reference, seek your advice and eventually help build your brand.

Pat's Tips:  If you create a Facebook user account as your community name, it is much easier to add followers on Pinterest and Instagram, since you can invite all your friends to follow you.

# About the Author

Patrick "Pat" Hopper is partner at OpenSystems Media, one of the largest print and online sources for hardware and software engineers.

Besides his day-to-day activities at his publishing company, he also runs Grosse Pointey, the largest source for news and events, in Grosse Pointe, Michigan.

He has over 5000 followers in his network, has spoken at numerous events and conferences.

To share your views on this book, email him at patrickmhopper@gmail.com

www.ingramcontent.com/pod-product-compliance
Lightning Source LLC
Chambersburg PA
CBHW041304180526
45172CB00003B/964